4/23

300

BONNARD

AND HIS ENVIRONMENT

Pierre Bonnard, 1944. © Henri Cartier-Bresson, Magnum

THE MUSEUM OF MODERN ART, NEW YORK, IN COLLABORATION WITH

BONNARD

AND HIS ENVIRONMENT

TEXTS BY JAMES THRALL SOBY, JAMES ELLIOTT, AND MONROE WHEELER

THE LOS ANGELES COUNTY MUSEUM OF ART AND THE ART INSTITUTE OF CHICAGO

DISTRIBUTED BY DOUBLEDAY & COMPANY, INC., GARDEN CITY, NEW YORK

©1964, The Museum of Modern Art
11 West 53 Street, New York, N.Y. 10019
Library of Congress Catalogue Card No. 64-7643
Printed in the U.S.A. by The Case-Hoyt Corp.,
Rochester, New York
Designed by
Mary Ahern and Joseph Bourke Del Valle

999
.B63
N4

PREFACE AND ACKNOWLEDGMEN

THIS PUBLICATION RECORDS a joint effort o
museums to present a new survey of one
greatest painters of our century in the three
cities of the United States.

Bonnard's first one-man show outside Fra
place in New York when de Hauke & Co
forty of his paintings in 1928, two years aft
come to America to serve on the Carnegi
tional Jury in Pittsburgh, from which
Mr. Duncan Phillips acquired the first of
Bonnards he and his gallery in Washi
possess. Bonnard was first shown at The
Modern Art two months after it opened
of his paintings were included in Alfr
Jr.'s exhibition, ''Painting in Paris,''
1930. The Art Institute of Chicago
work, with Vuillard's, in 1938. Los
see a major Bonnard exhibition for
when the present showing inaugurates
ings of the Los Angeles County Mus
It is the second Bonnard retrospec
at The Museum of Modern Art; th
1948, the year following the artist's
sponsored by The Cleveland Muse
was directed by John Rewald who
first comprehensive study of Bonna
this volume is still available, we ha
to provide a substitute for Mr. R
summing up of the artist's career
On behalf of the Trustees of the
ing museums, we wish to record
museums and individuals (listed
have graciously consented to p
tures for the long period requir
bition. We are indebted to the
for its official sponsorship of th
the Association Française d'A
artist's nephew, Mr. Charles
the Museum of Fontainebleau

CONTENTS

Cover for *L'Album d'estampes*
The Museum of Modern Art,

Entrance to *Le Bosquet*, Bonnard's home at Le Cannet, 1944. © Henri Cartier-
Bresson, Magnum

INTRODUCTION

It is a paradox of Pierre Bonnard's long and most distinguished career that in the United States, where the French impressionists found a number of early and fervent champions, their spiritual heir, Bonnard, has only lately come to great fame. His professional career began in the early 1890s, and yet for almost fifty years there was no public or private collection here where his works could be seen in number except in the Phillips Collection in Washington, D. C. Perhaps his art was too French for our taste, though this is hard to believe considering the fact that from the date of the Armory Show (1913) to the outbreak of World War II the School of Paris dominated the American art scene. Possibly our taste for visual revolution, once aroused, found Bonnard belated in aim. At any rate his following and patronage remained predominantly European until after the war. He was revered in Paris by colleagues we had long since taken to our hearts, yet we seemed unwilling to believe in their faith. As a case in point, in 1947 *Cahiers d'Art* in Paris published an article on Bonnard entitled "Pierre Bonnard—est-il un grand peintre?" The article concluded: "How to explain the reputation of Bonnard's work?... It is evident that this reverence is shared only by people who know nothing about the grave difficulties of art and cling above all to what is facile and agreeable." A stinging rebuttal was sent at once to the magazine by no less a world figure than Henri Matisse. Pierre Matisse tells me that he had seldom seen his father so angry.

Bonnard's art was of course the opposite of facile. It was painstaking and meditative to an extraordinary degree. One does not easily forget the story of Bonnard persuading his friend Vuillard to distract the guards in the Luxembourg Museum while he surreptitiously retouched one of his paintings which had been in the museum's collection for many years.

Bonnard's conscience was profound, his longing for perfection unrelenting. His instinctive modesty forced him to dislike personal flamboyance. He reserved daring—and it was often an extreme daring—for what he painted or drew. We have only begun to understand in this country what intimates like Vuillard and Matisse knew all along; namely, that a convinced flouting of conventions of color and form was quite as important a part of Bonnard's achievement as his unmistakable intimacy and charm. Once he looked intently at a picture by a predecessor and asked the owner of the gallery, "What do you want with a poor painting of mine, when you have in that canvas all that painting can be?" The picture in question was not by Claude Monet, to whose art of the later 1880s Bonnard's own seems most closely related. It was by Paul Cézanne. If Cézanne's influence on his younger countryman is impossible to determine precisely, the fact remains that the two men shared a mistrust of regimented values which some painters proclaim by abrupt defiance, others by quiet desertion from the ranks.

Girls. (c.1893). Pen and ink, 10 x 14".
Frank Perls Gallery, Beverly Hills, California

Circus Horse. (1946). Oil, 37 x 46 ½".
Private collection, Paris

When pondering the bolder aspects of Bonnard's art, I usually think first of his *Circus Horse*, completed the year before he died. In youth he had often painted horses, but for the most part they were ancient hacks drawing carriages along Paris' quieter streets. The muscular tensions of race-track thoroughbreds left him indifferent, whereas they had fascinated Degas and Lautrec. The truth is that Bonnard's basic domesticity of vision extended to almost all aspects of life in his time. And yet his *Circus Horse* is not easily dislodged from memory. It is opposite in spirit to the ghostly, malignant stallion which looms through the window in Fuseli's famous *Nightmare* of 1782. Nevertheless, its effect is scarcely less obsessive, the buffoonery of the horse's absurdly elongated head unforgettable. Bonnard's image proves again that great humor can strike at our consciousness nearly as hard as terror.

It would be an untenable exaggeration to refer to Bonnard as an *animalier* in the sense that the word was understood by earlier generations of artists. The fact remains that animals appear in his pictures repeatedly. His favorite was the small, affectionate dachshund which sidles into many of his composi-

tions and whose silhouette often acts as a complement to family relaxation. Bonnard was equally fond of cats. He liked them as beguiling pets and not for their capacity to become stand-ins for their jungle cousins, as did Delacroix. Bonnard was too late in time to share the Romantics' ardor for imperious steeds and for wild beasts caged in Paris zoos or running free in the African veldt. His interest was in animals to be held in the lap.

As already noted, Bonnard began to paint professionally in the early 1890s, as did his lifelong friend, Vuillard. It always comes as something of a shock to remember that Toulouse-Lautrec was so nearly the contemporary of these two artists; he was only three years older than Bonnard; he was Vuillard's elder by four. I assume our confusion arises from the fact that Lautrec has always been closely identified with *fin-de-siècle* esthetics, whereas his slightly junior colleagues have not. Lautrec outlived his astonishingly self-contained decade by a mere year.

Vuillard and Bonnard went on and on, the former with dwindling authority for the most part, the latter with uninterrupted ascendancy to the end of his long life. Like most good artists Bonnard had his vintage years. He almost never had one during which his creative yield was thin or bitter.

Bonnard and Vuillard were devoted friends throughout their long careers. Indeed there was a durability of affection and respect among leaders of their generation which exploded into recrimination with their successors in the School of Paris. In youth the two friends were allied in the movement called ''the Nabis''—the Hebrew word for prophets. As happens sporadically in art history, far less talented painters—Paul Sérusier and Maurice Denis —were the movement's most effective polemicists.

The Nabis met often, seeking the warmth of mutual aim and faith. In most accounts of their mildly insurrectionary gatherings Vuillard is described as restrained and rather morose, Bonnard as incurably gay. Members of the group had nicknames and Bonnard was known as ''the very Japanese Nabi'' because of his devotion to Oriental calligraphy in general and Japanese prints in particular. Later on, I think, the nickname took on a new and perhaps more profound meaning. For Bonnard was to emerge as a pearl diver among artists of his generation. In numerous works of his later career he discovered a nacreous quality in objects that the tides of familiarity had clouded or covered with habit's blind sand.

In youth Vuillard may well have been the more original of the two friends. He was apparently indifferent to or at least not deeply moved by the tonal subtleties of plane which were Cézanne's obsession. Instead, perhaps with Gauguin's more recent example in mind, he hung sheets of restrained and bland color one behind another and somehow kept them separate in air and space. I suppose his was essentially an intaglio process; I cannot think of any artist since who has used his system of pleated perspective, one stiff fold succeeding another as in an opened accordion, with his deftness and control. Vuillard's difficulty was that in later life he became cautious and precise to such a degree that one of his many celebrated portrait subjects asked her maid to remove some medicine from her bedside table ''because M. Vuillard paints everything he sees.''

Bonnard, on the contrary, grew more and more absorbed in fugitive and delicate forms of observation. These forms were once well described by Clive Bell, to my mind an underrated critic because of today's sometimes obtuse preference for architectonic, over-poetic, or sensual values. Bell wrote: ''There is something Chinese about him [Bonnard]; and he is one of those rare Europeans who have dealt in 'imposed' rather than 'built-up' design. Bonnard's pictures as a rule grow not as trees; they float as water lilies. European pictures, as a rule, spring upwards, masonry-wise, from their foundation; the design of a picture by Bonnard, like that of many Chinese pictures and Persian textiles, seems to have been laid on the canvas as one might lay cautiously on dry grass some infinitely precious figured gauze.''

After his youth as the friend in Paris of artists, writers, magazine editors, and impresarios of the stage, Bonnard spent most of his life in country houses throughout France. He tended to restrict his range of subject matter to daily scenes relating to life in the towns and resorts of his native land. He also restricted himself still further in the themes he chose. Whereas Vuillard as a bachelor had a lively interest in the salons of urbane houses where he was welcome as a distinguished guest, Bonnard preferred the rooms of family intimacy—the kitchen, the bedroom, the bath. In this preference he was the almost total opposite of Lautrec, who so disliked home life that he could hardly wait to bolt out the door and seek in hired warmth the affection his mother tried to give him and his monstrous father did his best to destroy.

Another recurrent element in Bonnard's iconography was related to his liking for uncomplicated domesticity. It was food. Not food as prepared by the great restaurants of France so much as food prepared at home by a skilled housewife or maid. He obviously loved the aromas of family kitchens. And in this connection there is a fact to be noted. Bonnard was apparently awed by the luminosity of the Dutch Little Masters, who were perpetually concerned with food and drink as subjects for their art. Yet whereas the seventeenth-century Hollanders liked to paint food on large tables, awaiting preparation, Bonnard was equally if not more interested in the feast itself. Though he often painted the separate ingredients of a fine luncheon or dinner, he seemed to be looking forward in imagination to the final repast. In 1910 or thereabouts, for example, he did a sumptuous picture called *La Bouillabaisse*. The components of the classic Mediterranean stew are assembled uncooked on a kitchen table, and a cat looks on voraciously. But the room is already pungent with the steam of the finished dish in its tureen. If the frail skin of onions and the shimmer of goblets are subjects that have fascinated artists for centuries, they have not often been given so

BRIEF CHRONOLOGY

1867 Born October 3, in Fontenary-aux-Roses, near Paris. His father came from the Dauphiné and headed an office in the War Ministry; his mother came from Alsace.

1877- Receives classical education at lycées de Vanves, Louis-le-
1887 Grand, and Charlemagne, and in Paris enters law school. Begins sketching.

1888 Curtails law studies to work at Ecole des Beaux-Arts and Académie Julian, where he meets Vuillard, Roussel, Denis, Vallotton, Ranson, and Sérusier. The latter, inspired by Gauguin, organizes his friends into a group called the "Nabis" (prophets).

1889- First studio: rue Le Chapelais. Military service at Bour-
1890 goile, where he meets the composer Claude Terrasse, whom Bonnard's sister soon marries. Receives 100 francs for champagne poster. Meets Toulouse-Lautrec. Shares studio with Vuillard and Denis, 28 rue Pigalle.

1891- Exhibits paintings at Salon des Indépendants and, with Nabis,
1894 at Le Barc de Boutteville's Gallery. Is discovered by critics Gustave Geffroy and Roger Marx. 1893: Makes poster, drawings, and lithographs for La Revue Blanche. Meets dealer Ambroise Vollard. Studio, 65 rue de Douai.

1895 Vollard publishes lithographs, Quelques aspects de la vie de Paris. Designs stained-glass window for Louis Comfort Tiffany.

1896 First one-man show, at Durand-Ruel's (49 paintings, prints, posters).

1897 In group show at Vollard's. Draws illustrations for Peter Nanson's Marie for La Revue Blanche. Vollard issues album of his lithographs.

1898 First showing abroad, with van Gogh, Gauguin, and Vuillard, in Oslo, Stockholm, and Göteborg.

1899 Bernheim-Jeune et Cie., becomes his dealer, a lifelong relationship. Visits Roussel often in L'Etang-la-ville. Studios: rue Le Chapelais and rue Ballu.

1900 Vollard publishes Verlaine's Parallèlment, with 109 lithographs and 9 wood engravings by Bonnard. In group exhibition at Bernheim-Jeune's.

1902 Vollard publishes Daphnis and Chloé, with 160 lithographs by Bonnard.

1903 Studio: 65 rue de Douai.

1904 One-man show at Bernheim-Jeune's, first of a dozen held at the gallery between 1904 and 1933. Draws 67 illustrations for Jules Renard's Histoires Naturelles.

1905- André Gide praises his paintings at the Salon d'Automne.
1906 Begins spending summers at Villennes and Vernouillet in the Seine Valley and Cotteville in Normandy.

1907 Paris studio: 60 rue de Douai. Between 1907 and 1911 takes short trips to Belgium, Holland, England, Italy, Spain, and Tunisia.

1908 Sale of Natanson collection, including 19 paintings by Bonnard which bring an average of 810 francs each.

1910 4 decorative panels for Missia Godebska shown at Salon d'Automne. Studios: 60 rue de Douai, 21 quai Voltaire.

1911 One-man show, Durand-Ruel's (27 paintings; also 3 decorative panels, later shown at Salon d'Automne).

1912 Buys small house, Ma Roulotte, at Vernonnet, near Vernon. Until 1938 divides time between Seine Valley and the south (Grasse, St. Tropez, Le Cannet). Paris studio: 22 rue Tourlaque.

1913 Travels in Holland and, with Vuillard, in England.

1914- During First World War lives mostly in Saint-Germain-
1918 en-Laye.

1919 First book on Bonnard, by Léon Werth. Paris address: 56 rue Molitor, Auteuil.

1922 Represented at Venice Biennale.

1923 Wins third prize, Carnegie International Exhibition, Pittsburgh.

1924 Retrospective exhibition at Gallery Druet, Paris (68 works).

1925 Marries his lifelong companion Marthe de Méligny (Maria Boursin). Buys villa Le Bosquet at Le Cannet. Paris residence: 48 Blvd. des Batignolles.

1926 To U.S.A. as juror for Carnegie International Exhibition.

1928 First one-man show outside France, at de Hauke & Co., New York (40 paintings).

1930 First showing at The Museum of Modern Art, New York (7 paintings in exhibition "Painting in Paris"). Vollard publishes his La Vie de Sainte Monique, with 29 drawings (transferred on stone), 17 etchings, and 178 compositions (drawn on wood), by Bonnard.

1932 Bonnard-Vuillard exhibition at Kunsthaus, Zurich. One-man exhibition at Galerie Braun et Cie., Paris (40 portraits). 1932-38: Summers in Deauville and Trouville; winters in Le Cannet.

1934 One-man show at Wildenstein's, New York (44 paintings).

1936 Wins second prize at Carnegie International Exhibition.

1938 Bonnard-Vuillard exhibition at The Art Institute of Chicago.

1939 Retrospective exhibition at Svensk-Franska Gallery,

Stockholm (51 paintings). After outbreak of war, Bonnard stays in Le Cannet.

1940 Death of Vuillard.

1942 Death of Madame Bonnard, January 26.

1945 Short visit to Paris.

1946 Retrospective exhibition at Bernheim-Jeune's (34 works). Consents to large retrospective at The Museum of Modern Art, New York, to celebrate his eightieth birthday.

1947 Death of Bonnard, January 23, in Le Cannet. The artist's nephew, Charles Terrasse, arranges large memorial exhibitions at the Carlsberg Glyptothek, Copenhagen; Stedelijk Museum, Amsterdam (77 works), and the Orangerie in Paris (197 works). Exhibition at Svensk-Franska Gallery, Stockholm (53 works).

1949 Exhibition, Kunsthaus, Zurich (247 works).

1950 Exhibition, Bernheim-Jeune's (62 works).

1951 Exhibition, Kunsthalle, Berne (76 works).

1953 Exhibition, Museum Boymans, Rotterdam (129 works).

1954 Exhibition, Lyon Musée (106 works).

1955 Exhibitions: Kunsthalle, Basel (173 works); Palazzo Reale, Milan (103 works); Musée des Ponchettes, Nice (78 works); Maison de la Pensée Française, Paris (45 works); "Bonnard, Vuillard et les Nabis, 1888-1903," Musée National d'Art Moderne, Paris.

1956 Exhibitions: Kunstverein, Brunswick, Germany (96 works); Bernheim-Jeune's (58 works).

Swan, illustration for *Histoires Naturelles* (p. 65). (1904). Brush and ink, 12 1/8 x 7 1/2". Collection Mr. and Mrs. Seth Dennis, Westport, Connecticut

BIOGRAPHICAL COMMENT

THE LIFE OF PIERRE BONNARD was extraordinarily private, with little dramatic incident and no major changes of vocation or destiny from beginning to end. Just as his lifework of painting has an essential continuity and homogeneity, his biography is all of a piece, and does not lend itself interestingly to narrative form. He himself was of little assistance as to particular problems of Bonnard scholarship; he did not remember such things precisely and, as a rule, did not even date his pictures.

His father was a government official of some importance in the War Ministry. Presumably to please him, in his early twenties Bonnard studied law, but simultaneously also went to art school. When it came time for his oral law examinations, he failed. After that he worked as a clerk in a government office for several months.

Then he sold a work of art: a color lithograph designed as a champagne poster for a Reims wine-merchant, for which he received a hundred francs. "A glorious event," as he recalled it years later; it emboldened him to declare to his father that he was not going to be able to become a lawyer or a bureaucrat; he was an artist. Presumably his family gave him some financial support during his novitiate. He soon began to sell his paintings, and less than a decade later signed an advantageous contract with an important dealer. His way of life was never extravagant; he seems never to have been troubled about money.

At twenty-eight he became intimate with a young woman who called herself Marthe de Méligny, although her name in fact was Maria Boursin; and their relationship (without marriage ceremony until 1925) went on uninterruptedly until her death. According to Bonnard's nephew, Charles Terrasse, it is she who appears in his pictures, early and late, more than anyone else: a woman of beautiful bodily proportions and peculiar grace, "fleeting and free, of which the great observer's eye would always catch a gesture, a movement, or an undulation in the light."

Thadée Natanson, one of the far-sighted early collectors of Bonnard's work, has described her even more graphically: "Close to him, in exiguous quarters, we saw fluttering that young woman, then still a child, with whom he spent his life. She already had, and kept always, her wild look of a bird, her movement on tiptoe, as though wingèd. . . ." She was somewhat neurotic, he suggests, "alarming everyone around her (and herself) about her health." Others who knew her have spoken of her self-absorption, verging on unfriendliness and isolation, and of the fanatic care she took of herself and her extreme cleanliness. And thus Bonnard painted her, at her ablutions, or as a haunting presence, sometimes almost unnoticeable in a corner or partly beyond the frame, peering into the picture.

The best description of Bonnard himself, in the prime of life, is also Natanson's: "This slim, active man seems tall, although he stoops a little and folds up on himself. . . . He strokes his short beard which curls loosely on his obstinate chin. . . . His near-sightedness is that of an observer, but it eliminates useless details. Behind his spectacles, unusually lively pupils glance at or fix upon successive objects, to make them his own."

He was physically strong, fond of bicyling and boating, and to the end of his life would always go for a walk before breakfast, as a devout man goes to mass. He was devout, in his own way, about landscape, ever-renascent light, and the spectrum in everything; these, indeed, were fundamentals of his lifework. To use an old formula of the philosophers, he put his faith in "the coherence of Nature and Art"; and, of course, in his experience and pictorial predilection, human nature was a part of the whole—indoors and outdoors constantly communicating.

Family Scene. 1893. Color lithograph, 12 ⅜ x 7 ⅛″.
The Museum of Modern Art, New York. Purchase

Aside from his vocation of painting there were two sides to his life: the enthralled and responsible lifelong marital relationship, and a physical restlessness which took him from place to place, sometimes abroad, but especially in France, with a true love of his native land in all its wonderfully differentiated parts. He always maintained a home base in Paris—nine addresses of studios and apartments are known to us—but as his life went on, he spent more and more of the year elsewhere, in the valley of the Seine, in Normandy, and in the Midi. During most of the war years, 1914-18, he more or less regularly spent the winters in the south of France, at Antibes, Cannes, Grasse, and St. Tropez and finally at Le Cannet, where in 1925 he bought the small Villa du Bosquet, on a hill overlooking Cannes. But he still moved about, summering at La Baule or Deauville or Arcachon; also frequenting various watering places at other seasons.

One reason for this mobility was Bonnard's enjoyment of motoring. In 1911 he acquired a ten horsepower Renault, and on his first excursion in it drove straight to Mont Saint-Michel. Thereafter he was a confirmed motorist. In 1912 when he bought a house in Vernonnet called "Ma Roulotte," his first improvement of it was the installation of a modern bathroom for Madame Bonnard; then he added a garage for himself. He was a leisurely driver, often covering as little as thirty miles a day, stopping frequently, sketching here and there, spending the night where convenient.

While he did not always work when he traveled, his eye for landscape never ceased to explore and accumulate pictorial material. Harry Lachman, an American painter, once invited him to go on a painting expedition across the Italian border. He arrived with all his own equipment: paintbox, canvases, portable easel. Bonnard, to his surprise, appeared on the threshold with no such impedimenta. Lachman had assumed that he was going to paint, but with what? Bonnard brushed this question aside, saying, as he seated himself contentedly in the car, "Moi, j'observe."

Except for Vuillard whom he always loved and admired, his relations with fellow painters were mutually respectful, cordial in some cases, but not close. His champagne poster impressed Toulouse-Lautrec, who sought him out and recommended his

Portrait. (c. 1893). Lithograph, 11 ½ x
9 ¾″, projected print for *L'Escarmouche*.
The Museum of Modern Art, New
York. Gift of Abby Aldrich Rockefeller

early pictures to prospective purchasers. Pissarro
on the other hand disliked his first exhibition, and
in a letter to his son declared that Monet and Renoir
shared his adverse opinion. They all came around to
a better appreciation of his talent later. Renoir in-
scribed to him two small paintings, which he would
show to visitors with pride and admiring comment.

One day late in his life, somewhat discontentedly
examining a painting by Rouault, he remarked to
Louis Carré, "Rouault wasn't as lucky as I. He
didn't know Renoir, who used to say to me, 'You
must beautify things, Bonnard, always beautify!' ''

He has been called the last of the impressionists—
and so described himself to Matisse—but of course
never followed in their footsteps exactly. But like
Renoir and like Matisse he was not afraid of its
being said that he painted too happily and decora-
tively. "One is not always transported with joy by
what one sees," he told Tériade, "but a painter
must be able to discern some agreeable connection
between one thing and another, and to find a place
for it in his painting. We can abstract beauty out of
everything." (bibl. 184)

Some of his pictures were completed in short
order, a matter of hours or days after he started
them; but as a rule he kept them in view a long
while and improved them little by little. Terrasse
tells us that, in his middle period, the greater part
of his work was begun while traveling around, but
finished in the studio. Often he made use of a single
great length of canvas which he affixed to the wall
wherever he happened to be, marking on it differ-
ent-sized areas for various pictures. At the end of
his sojourn he would roll it up, put it in his car, un-
roll it again when he got home, and later cut it up.

The longer he lived the more he concentrated on
color; stronger and stronger combinations of juxta-
posed or superimposed pigment. Sometimes, having mixed one of his burning hues, vermilion or
magenta or violet blue or peacock blue, and applied
it to the work in progress, he would wander around
the house from canvas to canvas, finding little places
where he could insert what he had left over. As he
himself said, a given color is very different when
you see it with other colors adjacent. André Girard
tells us that when Rouault retouched his pictures to
improve them he called it "Bonnard-ing." (bibl. 77)

In 1943 he told Angèle Lamotte that often, when
a painter gets to painting, what his picture portrays
is an embarrassment to him. "The point of depar-
ture for a work of art is an idea," and in the presence of his subject matter, there is always a danger
of the artist's becoming involved in immediacies
and incidentals. She then asked whether he never
painted with his subject before him. "Oh, yes, but
I leave it," he answered, "and come back to it later.

I never let myself become absorbed in the reality. . . . In fact there is always some conflict between the initial concept, which is the right one, the painter's own, and the varied and ever variable world. . . .'' (bibl. 184)

In every reality that seemed to him worth representing, he was struck by some aspect which perhaps no one else would have noticed. During the war he told André Suarès, "I've discovered peaches. They're so intense and soft, and some of them resemble a setting sun; only it's a sunset that does not disappear, which is most convenient for a painter.'' (bibl. 77)

He never imagined a picture in the abstract, but, on the other hand, he wanted the texture and substance of every square inch of his painting as such to be strong and sumptuous, though at the expense of recognizability. Upon occasion, concentrating to excess, he slipped into awkwardnesses, misrepresentations. He liked to have under his eyes in the studio any such exaggerated pictures. He said to

André Girard, "It is important to keep one's failures; they present problems that I find passionately interesting." (bibl. 77)

Though stubborn about such idiosyncracies, he would speak of them apologetically. Once he said to Emile Compard, a young painter of his acquaintance, "If you only knew what trouble I have drawing things!" and gave as an example the time someone had called his attention to the fact that, in a standing nude belonging to Félix Fénéon, he had given the figure two right feet. But he had not changed it. "After all, somehow, it seems to me better like that. It makes an interesting shape." (bibl. 264) Upon another occasion he said, "At times the faults in a picture are what give it life." (bibl. 184)

In some pictures he applied color until he achieved the dense effect of barbaric jewelry or oriental fabric. In others, even on a large scale, he kept to the thinness and rapidity of watercolor, often expressing a preference for a sketchier work. Compard

Boating. (c. 1897). Color lithograph, 10⁹⁄₁₆ x 18½". The Museum of Modern Art, New York. Gift of Abby Aldrich Rockefeller

proudly recalls the elder painter's wanting to acquire one of his pictures. "Would you like me to pay for it," Bonnard asked, "or shall we make an exchange?" Wisely, Compard preferred a Bonnard, no matter how slight, to his own current market price, and finally had to choose between a small basket of green gages or a small nude. He decided on the nude. "Bravo!" cried Bonnard. "In the still life I have worked over the paint, whereas the nude is only a sketch. But I like a canvas not to look wearied by the brush." (bibl. 264)

In the chosen picture, he went on to say, he had expressed what he had in mind, then stopped. "I couldn't have given it another touch, which is rare for me," he added laughingly. "I always carry in my pocket a little box with some colors ready in it. When I come across one of my canvases that displeases me, out comes my little box, and I fix it." In his old age he confessed to Girard that, in his opinion, his pictures still lacked "form, accent, and a skeleton. . . . I am just beginning to understand what it is to paint. A painter should have two lives, one in which to learn, and one in which to practice his art." (bibl. 77)

The German occupation in the late spring of 1940 scattered most of Bonnard's Paris friends; Vuillard died in June; and thereafter Bonnard preferred to stay in the south of France the year round. Madame Bonnard died on January 6, 1942. At the end of the war he returned to the metropolis for a while, but it no longer suited him. He went back to Le Cannet, and there the end came on January 23, 1947.

Laundry Girl. (1896). Charcoal, 12 ¼ x 7 ¾".
Private collection, Paris

The Laundry Girl. 1896. Color lithograph,
11 ⅝ x 7 ⅞".
The Museum of Modern Art, New York.
Gift of Victor S. Riesenfeld

The close of Bonnard's life was marked by a singular incident having to do with the inheritance of his pictures. When at last he married Marthe de Méligny, on August 13, 1925, it was according to a provision of French law called "communauté des biens"—joint ownership. She had always given him to understand that she had no living relatives; it was only when he married her that he learned her real name. She never made a will. After her death he found to his dismay and distress that, as a consequence of her intestacy, all his work would have to be listed and appraised and placed under seal.

Resenting the formalities of law involved—under the misleading advice of a lawyer, and confident that he was not acting to anyone's disadvantage—he drew up a will in her behalf, bequeathing to himself what surely belonged to him morally. He signed the will with her name, but did not attempt to disguise his own handwriting, and ingenuously even dated it six months after her death. Nevertheless, it was accepted by the local authorities, and thus he was able to conclude his life serenely, with no further uneasiness about the paintings in his possession.

As it happened, he possessed a great many. Both he and Vuillard had enjoyed a certain success prior to the First World War and had saved money, which dwindled to nothing in the inflation of the twenties. Whereupon they decided that, in lieu of other investments, they would simply keep a part of their artistic production.

The irregularity of Bonnard's situation inevitably came to light after his death, when it was discovered that Madame Bonnard had four nieces. At first it seemed possible that the entire estate might go to these ladies, because of the falsification of the will. A difficult sequence of litigations ensued, concluded by a compromise sixteen years later, when the pictures were divided between Bonnard's own family and his wife's.

MONROE WHEELER

Young Girl with Black Stockings. (1893). Lithograph, 11 7/16 x 5 1/16", published in *L'Escarmouche*, January 14, 1894. The Museum of Modern Art, New York. Gift of Abby Aldrich Rockefeller

21

BONNARD AND HIS ENVIRONMENT

PIERRE BONNARD DIED IN 1947, and since that time the recognition of his greatness has spread in widening circles. Along with this recognition has come the realization that his vision far transcended the charm and intimacy for which it received early praise. In seemingly gentle investigations of a modest environment, Bonnard produced works of art that are both monumental and lyrical, works that expand the insight as well as the formal devices of the impressionists in a profound and original way. His evolution offers an extended and natural transition from impressionism to abstraction that omits, or appears to omit, everything in between.

Bonnard never repudiated or openly defied the conventional French milieu in which he grew up. Living on his own terms behind a screen of charm and nonchalance, following his own path with quiet tenacity, he celebrated both in his life and in his art the amusements and tranquil pleasures of French middleclass life. It was a life in which gratification of the senses was easily accepted. The hedonism that pervades the world of his art, however, is a moderate hedonism, which he presents (especially in interior scenes) with a questioning undertone. Although in his early work he chides his milieu for its foibles with a sly but affectionate wit, in his later paintings there is greater sympathy with bourgeois life, but never uncritical sympathy.

Bonnard seldom recorded acts or events. His concern was with the feelings—the ''poetry,'' as he called it—evoked by the things he knew best, and because he favored these subjects, he was even early in his career called an *intimist* painter. But one of the puzzling aspects of Bonnard's art is the detachment in the way the near and the familiar are approached. Often, for example, the people portrayed seem to be only incidentally present in the scene and only remotely conscious of their surroundings. Even the figures given prominence rarely seem

L'Estampe et l'Affiche, poster. (c. 1896).
Color lithograph, 32 x 23 ½".
The Museum of Modern Art, New York. Purchase

to be aware of the artist or of one another. They are absorbed in themselves, or their attention is averted. This is particularly true of the nudes, sensuously painted as they are. When the attention of an individual is directed toward anything, it is usually toward an animal, a child, or an object. Between adults there is psychological distance, and close physical association only adds an ambiguous tension to it. Bonnard cunningly evokes doubtful and unresolved aspects of human relationship: nostalgia, indifference, wistfulness.

In spite of the initial impression one might get to the contrary, the situations portrayed are not specific. The poses and gestures are the inevitable movements of people doing ordinary things, part of a continuum rather than fixed in crucial moments. With this emphasis on the transient nature of experience is an atmosphere that is hauntingly enigmatic.

The world of Bonnard's art—although it is domestic and pastoral as well as urban—no longer seems to belong to the nineteenth century. It contains too much playful irony and, in later stages, too much melancholy and even apprehensiveness. It shows a range of feeling far wider than that with which it is often credited. Although the choice of imagery seems narrow, the interpretation and expression—the pictorial results—vary the way human feeling itself varies under the slow yet urgent pressures of life.

But while Bonnard may have been passive in his choice of subject, his art was the active, transforming agent of a searching sensibility and mind. He explored color and the effects and clues that determine the perception of both actual and painted objects and nature. In looking at his paintings, especially those done after 1915, one is often initially puzzled by the shape of an object, by an action, or by the definition of space. One has to take time to relate the visual information to physical facts, to associate the disparate painted clues with reality, and to familiarize oneself with the particular conception of each picture—even while on first impression one may be enchanted with the color, amused by the unexpected composition, or as is sometimes the case, disappointed with the whole effect. One readily accepts the familiar subjects with their pleasant associations, but once involved with them one finds that Bonnard also offers new pictorial interpretations of visual experience that push representational art to new limits.

Born in 1867, Bonnard came to artistic maturity in the ebullient, fermenting Paris of the 1890s. As one of the Nabis he was quickly among the avant-garde and was influenced by Gauguin and Japanese art. His association with the Nabis, however, was easygoing, based more on personal friendship than on adherence to any program or militant theory of subject or style. The ideas dominating advanced French painting in the 1890s produced several anti-naturalistic currents with decorative tendencies, and not unexpectedly, Bonnard's early style belongs to such currents—especially art nouveau. But no matter how decorative his arabesques and flat patterns, Bonnard still infused them with an amazing feeling of playful life and vivid suggestions of personality. That same sense of life he put into every manner in which he worked. He borrowed easily and openly at a time when his fellow artists quarreled fiercely over influences. Bonnard did not worry about reputation; he was too confident in his art.

There were many seeming contradictions in Bonnard. Even in his paintings, facility and elegance of style are combined with a touch that is at times graceless; innocence is combined with sensuousness; the conservative, with the experimental. His pictures offer unconventional perspectives, puzzles, and the surprise of hidden details. In personality he was diffident, but also brilliant, lighthearted, and boyish. Yet in his own unobtrusive way, he remained independent and self-possessed in his art

Place Clichy. (c. 1923). Color lithograph, 18 ⅝ x 25 3/16″.
Lent by The Art Institute of Chicago

Woman Opening Door. (1941). Pencil, 25 ½ x 19 ¾".
Private collection, Paris

from beginning to end. Although he followed the rapid subsequent changes in French art of his day—fauvism, cubism, dadaism, surrealism, and abstraction—with interest, he remained apart from them. In his own way of painting, however, there was a wide variety at any given time.

Bonnard's evolution also embodied paradoxes. Although in the 1890s he was very much a post-impressionist, he had begun to gravitate toward impressionism before the close of the decade, slowly turning back to a naturalism which he sensed still had unexplored expressive possibilities. After 1900 he paid even more attention to nature, becoming increasingly concerned with space and light, and especially with color. It was then that Bonnard assimilated into his own style technical means of the impressionists—short brush strokes, lighter tonal values, sophisticated hue relationships.

Around the beginning of World War I, however, Bonnard seriously questioned the direction in which his interest in nature and impressionism had taken him. He felt he had been carried away by a passion for color and had unconsciously sacrificed form. He began to draw constantly to strengthen form and worked with a new emphasis on composition. At the same time he also developed his use of higher-keyed color, employing it with a renewed sense of the two-dimensional in an unexpected reprise of the decorative aims of his first paintings. The changes that followed took him close to abstraction after 1920 and were based on an unhurried merging of his lyric naturalism with an increasingly monumental decorative goal, which resulted in the spectacular achievements of the last three decades of his life, when he produced his greatest paintings.

Bonnard worked, as he said, with "a brush in one hand, a rag in the other." He did not paint directly from the subject, but from memory, small sketches, and brief color notations. He began with a "first idea," which was usually realized over a long period of time, in a way related to the time required to "read" the finished painting. Angel Zarraga, a Mexican artist who had the opportunity to watch Bonnard at work in a hotel room at Cap d'Antibes, probably during the mid-1920s, gives the following description of Bonnard at work:

> . . . on the walls hung canvases of various sizes and proportions. During my first visit all the canvases were white. The whole room radiated from them. When I came back a few days later, I saw on every one of them a few colorful accents whose pictorial meaning was not at all recognizable. I guessed in part what Bonnard then explained to me. When he begins a picture his composition is not immediately established. . . . He simply walks back and forth between the white surfaces, waits for an idea, sets here a tone, there a brush stroke, puts several streaks on a third canvas. After a little while . . . he lays down his brush, calls his dog, who is always near . . . and goes for a walk with him on the beach. He chats for fifteen minutes or a half hour with acquaintances he meets and then abruptly,

but gently, he breaks off the conversation and returns quickly to his room. Seemingly at random, he sets down here and there, on one picture and another, a few accents which had meanwhile become clear to him and then goes for another walk in order to relax and gather his energies for another attack. Weeks, even months pass in this way. With great astonishment I saw what emerged. . . . Three months later I was again in his room. . . . On the walls I saw half a dozen finished and wonderfully resolved pictures. Before every single one I thought: This was created in a couple of hours, in a hasty mood and with playful ease. 'As for me, I do not know how to invent,' he said to me. He who, one feels, has invented everything! (bibl. 9)

Bonnard was essentially a colorist. He devoted his main creative energies to wedding his sensations of color from nature to those from paint itself—sensations which he said thrilled and even bewildered him. Perceiving color with a highly developed sensitivity, he discovered new and unfamiliar effects from which he selected carefully, yet broadly and audaciously. Sometimes he chose bright, clearly contrasted harmonies of hue, but more often he sought nuances and delicately modulated transitions. Whether in narrow range or multitudinous variety, the colors move across the surface of his paintings in constantly shifting interplay, lending an extraordinary fascination to common subjects. Familiar sights—the pervading greenness of a landscape, the intensification of color in objects on a lightly overcast day—are given vivid life. Sights which escape normal attention are isolated for our pleasure: the detailed changes of planes at the edges of windows are described in many bands of color; shadows cast by objects partially lost in the glare of a strong overhead light are given material substance. New experiences are opened up, as when the chromatic sensations conveyed are like those experienced by mystics or those induced by hallucinatory drugs. As time went on, Bonnard became increasingly daring and original in his use of intense colors and turned it to new expressive ends.

But he did not seek brightness alone. He also worked boldly with contrasts of value—light and dark. Of all the possible combinations of values and colors, he cherished especially the power in combinations of unfamiliar intermediate tones. He used them to record the subtle gradations in a world of half-lights, enhancing them by unexpectedly bright daubs and neighboring tones. In his works irregular juxtapositions of color and tone, ranging from near discordances to tender harmonies, hold the eye entranced. He records the strange illumination just before a storm, the light of predawn and evening: moments of uneasiness, anticipation, and nostalgia. He probed the limits of color experience and discovered wonders seemingly beyond the natural.

Above all, he used his singular effects of light and color to help establish mood. And the moods he cap-

Portrait of Girl. (c.1942-43). Pencil, 26 x 19 ¾″. Private collection, Paris

Children in Garden. (1908). Oil, 19 x 25″. Collection Mr. and Mrs. Lester Avnet, Kings Point, New York

OPPOSITE: *Repas des bêtes.* (C.1906). Oil, 29 x 42″. Collection Mr. and Mrs. Hugo Moser, New York

Regatta. (1908-12). Oil, 28 ⅝ x 39 ¾". Museum of Art, Carnegie Institute, Pittsburgh

OPPOSITE: *Tree near the River.* (c.1912). Oil, 40 x 31 ¾". Sonja Henie's and Niels Onstad's Collection, Los Angeles

Woman with Basket of Fruit. (1915-18). Oil, 26 ¾ x 15 ⅜". The Baltimore
Museum of Art, Cone Collection

OPPOSITE: *The Table.* (1925). 40½ x 29¼". The Trustees of The Tate Gallery, London

LEFT: *Still Life* (*La Table garnie*). (c.1924). Oil, 15 x 22". The Art Gallery of Toronto

The Dining Room at Le Cannet. (1924). Oil, 24 x 22½". Collection Mr. and Mrs. Clifford W. Michel, New York

Bouquet at Vernon. (c.1925). Watercolor, 25⅝ x 19⅝". Private collection, New York

Inter.

42   46

LEFT: *The Three Bouquets.* (1930). Oil, 22 ¾ x 23 ½".
Collection Mr. and Mrs. André Meyer, New York

Baskets of Fruit in Sun. (c.1927). Oil, 23 ¾ x 17 ¼".
Collection Mr. and Mrs. Theodore E. Cummings,
Beverly Hills, California

Landscape (La Grande vue de Vernon). (1929). Oil, 42 ¼ x 51 ½". Collection Mr. and Mrs. Alex M. Lewyt, New York

The Road to Nantes. (C.1930). Oil, 27 ¼ x 25 ⅞". The Cleveland Museum of Art, Leonard C. Hanna, Jr. Collection

OPPOSITE: *Bowl of Fruit.* (C.1933). Oil, 22 ¾ x 20 ¾". Philadelphia Museum of Art, Lisa Norris Elkins Collection

Dining Room on the Garden. (c.1933). Oil, 50⅛ x 53½″. The Solomon R. Guggenheim Museum, New York

OPPOSITE: *Table with Music Album.* (1926-32). Oil, 47¾ x 35¾″. Private collection, New York

Table before Window. (1943). Oil, 40 x 28½". Collection Edward A. Bragaline, New York

OPPOSITE: *View from Window.* (C. 1936-38). Crayon,
13 x 19¼". Private collection, New York

The Sea. (c.1944). Watercolor, 11 x 10¼".
Private collection, New York

Boulevard des Batignolles. (1900). Oil, 11 ⅝ x 15 ¾". Collection Mrs. Mellon Bruce, New York

The Bridge. (c.1908). Oil, 27 x 38″. Collection Mr. and Mrs. Sidney F. Brody, Los Angeles

OPPOSITE: *The Brothers Jean and Gaston Bernheim. 1920. Oil, 65 x 61". Musée National d'Art Moderne, Paris*

Dressing Table and Mirror. (C.1920). Oil, 48 ⅞ x 43". Collection Mr. and Mrs. Gustave M. Berne, Great Neck, N. Y.

Still Life (Coin de table). (c.1935). Oil, 26 ⅜ x 25″. Musée National d'Art Moderne, Paris

The Bottle of Red Wine. 1942. Oil, 26 x 24″. Collection Mr. and Mrs. Ralph F. Colin, New York

Flowering Almond Tree. (1946).
Oil, 21 ⅝ x 14 ⅜".
Musée National d'Art Moderne, Paris

LENDERS TO THE EXHIBITION:

Mr. and Mrs. Lester Avnet, Kings Point, New York; Roland Balaÿ, New York; Mr. and Mrs. Walter Bareiss; Mr. and Mrs. Gustave M. Berne, Great Neck, New York; Mr. and Mrs. Leigh B. Block, Chicago; Edward A. Bragaline, New York; Mr. and Mrs. Sidney F. Brody, Los Angeles; Mrs. Mellon Bruce, New York; Mr. and Mrs. Ralph F. Colin, New York; Mr. and Mrs. Theodore E. Cummings, Beverly Hills, California; Mr. and Mrs. Seth Dennis, Westport, Connecticut; Mr. and Mrs. Charles W. Engelhard, Far Hills, New Jersey; Mr. and Mrs. Jacques Gelman, Mexico City; Mr. and Mrs. William Goetz, Los Angeles; Lauder Greenway, New York; Mrs. Frank J. Gould, Cannes; Mr. and Mrs. William B. Jaffe, New York; Silvan Kocher, Solothurn, Switzerland; Mr. and Mrs. Alex M. Lewyt, New York; Wright Ludington, Santa Barbara, California; Mr. and Mrs. André Meyer, New York; Mr. and Mrs. Clifford W. Michel, New York; Mr. and Mrs. Hugo Moser, New York; Sonja Henie's and Neils Onstad's Collection, Los Angeles; The Lazarus Phillips Family Collection, Montreal; The Reader's Digest Association, Pleasantville, New York; Edward G. Robinson, Los Angeles; Mr. and Mrs. John D. Rockefeller 3rd, New York; Mrs. Walter Ross, New York; Professor William Rubin, New York; Mrs. Wolfgang Schoenborn, New York; Mr. and Mrs. Norton Simon, Los Angeles; James Thrall Soby, New Canaan, Connecticut; Mr. and Mrs. Donald S. Stralem, New York; Mrs. Lloyd Bruce Wescott, Rosemont, New Jersey; Mr. and Mrs. Charles Zadok, New York

The Baltimore Museum of Art; The Art Institute of Chicago; The Cleveland Museum of Art; The Tate Gallery, London; Milwaukee Art Center; The Minneapolis Institute of Arts; The Solomon R. Guggenheim Museum, New York; The Metropolitan Museum of Art, New York; The Museum of Modern Art, New York; Smith College Museum of Art, Northampton, Massachusetts; Musée National d'Art Moderne, Paris; Musée du Petit Palais, Paris; Philadelphia Museum of Art; Museum of Art, Carnegie Institute, Pittsburgh; Nationalmuseum, Stockholm; The Art Gallery of Toronto; Galleria Internazionale d'Arte Moderna, Venice; The Phillips Collection, Washington, D.C.

M. Knoedler & Co., Inc., New York; Frank Perls Gallery, Beverly Hills, California; Wildenstein & Co., Inc., New York.

CATALOGUE OF THE EXHIBITION

The Museum of Modern Art, New York:
October 7—November 29, 1964
The Art Institute of Chicago:
January 8—February 28, 1965
Los Angeles County Museum of Art:
March 31—May 30, 1965

Bonnard himself attached little importance to dates, as he sometimes worked on a picture over a period of many years; therefore, it is impossible to date many of his works with any degree

of assurance. Discrepancies as wide as fifteen years exist between the estimates of the most informed students. We have, therefore, listed the dates commonly agreed upon, even though future research will inevitably alter certain of them.

Dates in parentheses do not appear on the work. In dimensions height precedes width.

PAINTINGS

1. *Woman with Rabbit.* 1891. Oil on canvas, 37¾ x 17″. Collection Professor William Rubin, New York. Ill. p. 65.

2. *The Croquet Game.* 1892. Oil on canvas, 50¾ x 63½″. Private collection, Paris. Ill. p. 66.

3. *Screen (Promenade des nourrices, frise des fiacres).* (c. 1892-94). Distemper on unprimed canvas; four panels, each 58 x 17¾″. Private collection, New York. Ill. p. 31.

4. *Children Leaving School.* (c.1893). Tempera on cardboard, 11⅜ x 17½″. Collection Lauder Greenway, New York. Ill. p. 30.

5. *The Cottet Family.* 1894. Oil on wood, 13¾ x 10⅝″. M. Knoedler & Co., Inc., New York. Ill. p. 30.

6. *Street Scene with Two Dogs (Rue à Éragny-sur-Oise).* (1895). Oil on composition board, 13⅞ x 10⅝″. Collection Mr. and Mrs. Jacques Gelman, Mexico City. Ill. p. 32.

7. *Roof Tops.* (c.1895-1900). Oil on cardboard, 13½ x 15″. Smith College Museum of Art, Northampton, Massachusetts. Gift of The Adele R. Levy Fund, Inc. Ill. p. 32.

8. *The Bridge at Chatou.* (c.1896). Oil on wood, 12½ x 23½″. Private collection, New York. Ill. p. 33.

9. *Madame Terrasse and Her Children.* 1898. Oil on cardboard, mounted on wood, 13 x 10½″. Collection Mrs. Mellon Bruce, New York. Ill. p. 33.

10. *Interior.* (1898). Oil on cardboard, 20½ x 13¾″. Collection Mr. and Mrs. Norton Simon, Los Angeles. Ill. p. 67.

11. *Les Champs-Elysées.* (c.1898). Oil on board, 20½ x 30″. Private collection, Lausanne. Ill. p. 35.

12. *Boulevard des Batignolles.* (1900). Oil on wood, 11⅝ x 15¾″. Collection Mrs. Mellon Bruce, New York. Ill. p. 68.

13. *Place Blanche.* (c.1902). Oil on paper, mounted on wood, 23½ x 31¼″. Collection Edward G. Robinson, Los Angeles. Ill. p. 34.

14. *Girl in a Straw Hat.* (1903). Oil on canvas, 15 x 17½″. Milwaukee Art Center Collection. Gift of Harry Lynde Bradley. Ill. p. 35.

15. *The Terrasse Family.* (c.1904). Oil on canvas, 42½ x 49⅝″. Private collection, Paris. Ill. p. 70.

16. *Repas des bêtes.* (c.1906). Oil on canvas, 29 x 42″. Collection Mr. and Mrs. Hugo Moser, New York. Ill. p. 36.

17. *The Bridge.* (c.1908). Oil on canvas, 27 x 38″. Collection Mr. and Mrs. Sidney F. Brody, Los Angeles. Ill. p. 69.

18. *Children in Garden.* (1908). Oil on canvas, 19 x 25″. Col-

288 PHILLIPS, DUNCAN. Pierre Bonnard. *Kenyon Review* 2 no. 4: 561-566 ill. (col.) Autumn 1949.
Reprinted in bibl.127.

289 NATANSON, THADÉE. Le Bonnard que je propose. *Art-Documents* no. 1:7 ill. Oct. 1950.
Extract from bibl.12.

290 PERRUCHOT, HENRI. L'affaire Bonnard. *L'Oeil* no. 21:10-15 ill. Oct. 1958.
Similar coverage: L'affaire Bonnard. *Connaissance des Arts* no. 9:18-19 ill. 1952.—Le procès Bonnard. *Arts* no. 311: 1, 4 May 18, 1951.

291 OMAGGIO A BONNARD. *Emporium* 107 no. 638:50-57 ill. Feb. 1948.
Critiques on the Orangerie retrospective.

292 PIA, PASCAL. Ambroise Vollard, marchand et éditeur. *L'Oeil* no. 3:18-27 ill. 1955.

293 ROH, FRANZ. Bonnards Wunder der Farbe. *Kunst* 51:161-164 ill. 1952-53.

294 RUHEMANN, HELMUT. Methods of the masters, III: Five modern masters. *Studio* 145:72-77 ill. 1953.

295 SALOMON, JACQUES. Mon ami Bonnard. *Arts* no. 797:8 ill. Nov. 23-29, 1960.

296 SELVIG, FORREST. Les Nabis: prophets of the vanguard. *Art News* 61:34-37, 64-66 Dec. 1962.
On exhibit at the Minneapolis Institute.

297 SOBY, JAMES T. Last of the Impressionists: Pierre Bonnard. *Town & Country* 102:70-71, 90, 92, 94 ill. (col.).

298 STRALEM, JEAN & DONALD. The Nabis and their circle. *Minneapolis Institute Bulletin* 51:129-134 Dec. 1962.
Includes chronology, catalogue of exhibition, bibliography. Also note bibl. 95, 102.

299 SUTTON, DENYS. The "Revue Blanche." *Signature* (n.s.) no. 18:21-43 ill. 1954.
Includes brief French text by Natanson on Bonnard (Jan. 15, 1896). Also see Sutton's "Bonnard and his French contemporaries," *Burlington Magazine* June 1947.

300 TERRASSE, CLAUDE. Bonnard. *Art News Annual* 28:84-107, 32 ill. (12 col.) 1959.

301 THOMÉ, J. R. Pierre Bonnard (1867-1947), graveur et illustrateur. *Courrier Graphique* 24 no. 105:3-10 ill. Sept.-Oct. 1959.

302 TOWNDRON, KENNETH R. French painters, II: Bonnard. *Apollo* 55:79-83 ill. 1952.
On current London show.

303 WALDVOGEL, MELVIN. The Nabis and their circle, 1890-1900. *Art International* 7 no. 1:55-58 Jan. 25, 1963.
On exhibit at Minneapolis, Nov. 15-Dec. 30.

304 WALDVOGEL, MELVIN. Bonnard and Vuillard as lithographers. *Minneapolis Institute Bulletin* 52:66-81 Sept. 1963.
Bibliography.

305 WERTH, LÉON. Pierre Bonnard, illustrateur. *Portique* no. 7:9-20 ill. 1950.
"Essai de bibliographie des ouvrages illustrés par Pierre Bonnard," p. 19-20.

306 [ZERVOS, CHRISTIAN]. Liste des principales oeuvres françaises au Musée d'Art Moderne Occidental à Moscou. *Cahiers d'Art* 25 no.2:337 1950.
No. 1-14:Bonnard.

EXHIBITION CATALOGUES

307 BASEL. KUNSTHALLE. Pierre Bonnard. May 28-July 17, 1955. [60]p. 28 ill.
173 exhibits. Texts by R. T. Stoll and Charles Terrasse. Chronology, bibliography. Reviewed *Werk* 42:166 (suppl.) Aug. 1956.

308 BERNE, KUNSTHALLE. Der Maler der Revue Blanche. Mar. 21-Apr. 22, 1951.
No. 1-76 by Bonnard. Texts by Fritz Hermann, Arnold Rüdlinger. Chronology. Bibliography by Hans Bolliger. Complemented by: Estampes des Peintres de la "Revue blanche." Berne, Gutekunst & Klipstein, 1952. (Sales catalogue no. 50).

309 BOSTON. MUSEUM OF FINE ARTS. The Artist and the Book in Western Europe and the United States, 1860-1960. Boston, The Museum; Cambridge, Harvard College, 1961. Exhibited at Boston, May 4-July 16. Bonnard, p. 24-27 (ill.). Introduction by Philip Hofer; research and compilation by Eleanor M. Garvey and others. General bibliography.

310 BRUNSWICK. KUNSTVEREIN. Pierre Bonnard. Braunschweig, Nov. 11-Dec. 16, 1956. 40 p. incl. 28 pl. (col.).
Bibliography. Exhibit also shown at Bremen, Cologne.

311 BRUSSELS. PALAIS DES BEAUX ARTS. Le Mouvement symboliste. Jan. 31, 1956—Mar. 3, 1957.
Published by Éditions de la Connaissance. Bonnard, p. 133 (index). Exhibit on the cultural situation, including works of art, documents, editions. Prefaces by G. Bauer, R. Guiette.

312 EDINBURGH. ROYAL SCOTTISH ACADEMY. Exhibition of Paintings by Pierre Bonnard & Edouard Vuillard. Aug. 17-Sept. 18, 1948.
Published by the Arts Council of Great Britain. 55 exhibits by Bonnard (9 ill.), also 11 lithographs. "Last of the impressionists, called in the nineties *Symbolistes, Synthétistes, Intimistes, Classicistes, Idéistes . . .*"

313 LONDON. MARLBOROUGH LTD. Roussel, Bonnard, Vuillard. May 5-June 12, 1954.
No. 34-59 by Bonnard (8 ill.). Preface by John Russell. Varied texts including G. Geffroy on Bonnard (1896), also Signac, Denis, Gide. Chronology, bibliography. For review of later Bonnard exhibition see M. Amaya in *Apollo* 77:49 ill. Jan. 1963.

314 LYON. MUSÉE. Bonnard. Festival de Lyon-Charbonniers, 1954. 53p. incl. 17 ill.
Catalogue of 106 exhibits by M. Rocher-Jauneau with critical notes. Text by Charles Terrasse, René Jullian. Chronology, bibliography.

315 MILAN. ENTE MANIFESTAZIONI MILANESI. Pierre Bonnard. Apr.-May 1955. 78p. 66pl. (col.).
Catalogue of 103 exhibits and essay by Franco Russoli. Foreword by L. Morandi. Essay by Charles Terrasse (also in French). Bibliography, p.74-78. Shown also in Basel and Nice. Edition published by Silvana (Milano). Reviewed in *Arte Lombardo* 2:203-205 1956, *Arti* no. 1:I-IV, 6-22 1955, *Biennale di Venezia* no. 204:42-43 1955, *Domus*, no.309:48-49 1955, *Emporium* 121:265-272 1955.

316 NICE. MUSÉE DES PONCHETTES. Bonnard. Aug.-Sept. 1955. 44p. ill.

    Lists 78 exhibits. Preface by Charles Terrasse. Edited by Madeleine Guynet-Pechadre. Bibliography. Reviewed *Arts* (Paris) no. 532:8 Sept. 7-13, 1955.

317 PARIS. BERNHEIM-JEUNE & CIE. Exposition rétrospective: Bonnard. May-July 1950. 24p. ill.

    62 exhibits. Preface by Charles Terrasse. For later "Hommage à Bonnard" see *Studio* 152:91 Sept. 1956.

318 PARIS. MAISON DE LA PENSÉE FRANÇAISE. Bonnard. June 1955. 18 ill.

    Introduction by Georges Besson. Reviewed in *Arts (Paris)* no. 522:511 ill. June 29-July 5, 1955, *Art News* 54:47 Sept. 1955.

319 PARIS. MUSÉE NATIONAL D'ART MODERNE. Bonnard, Vuillard et les Nabis, 1888-1903. June 8-Oct. 2, 1955. 109p. 24 ill.

    Catalogue by Bernard Dorival and Agnès Humbert published by Éditions des Musées Nationaux (1955). Reviewed in *Arts (Paris)* no.520:14-21 June 1955, *Burlington Magazine* 97:267 Aug. 1955, *Emporium* 122:218-224 1955.

320 PARIS. MUSÉE DE L'ORANGERIE. Exposition Bonnard. Catalogue. 2.éd. Paris, Éditions des Musées Nationaux, 1948. 24p. ill.

    First edition for show held Oct.-Nov. 1947.

321 ROTTERDAM. MUSEUM BOYMANS. Bonnard. 1953. 16p. 36 ill.

    129 exhibits. Introduction by Charles Terrasse in Dutch and French. Chronology.

322 VENICE. ESPOSIZIONE BIENNALE INTERNAZIONALE D'ARTE. XXV. Catalogo. 1950.

    Bonnard section, with essay by Raymond Cogniat, p.285-286. Critique by Bernard Dorival in *Biennale di Venezia* no. 1:18-22 1950.

323 WASHINGTON. PHILLIPS GALLERY. Six Paintings by Bonnard. Jan. 12-Feb. 12, 1958. 12 ill.

    "A loan exhibition" with text by Duncan Phillips. Titled "A bulletin," the essay is reprinted from bibl.92.

324 WILLIAMSTOWN (Mass.). STERLING AND FRANCINE CLARK INSTITUTE. Exhibition 24: Pierre Bonnard Lithographs. Aug. 1963.

    19 exhibits (18pl.). Reviewed *American Artist* 27:8 Oct. 1963.

325 ZURICH. EIDGENOSSISCHE TECHNISCHE HOCHSCHULE. Bonnard-Vuillard: Handzeichnungen, Druckgraphik. Feb. 23-Apr. 27, 1952. 17p. cover ill.

    No catalogue listing, only "Einfuhrung von Erwin Gradmann." Reviewed in *Kunst und Volk* 14:39 1952, *Werk* 39 no. 4:48 (suppl.) Apr. 1952.

326 ZURICH. KUNSTHAUS. Pierre Bonnard, 1867-1947. June 6-July 24 1949. 38p. ill.

    247 exhibits. Texts by J. Leymarie and W. Wartmann in French and German. Reviewed in *Kunst und Volk* 11 no. 3: 72-74 1949, *Werk* 36:107 (suppl.) Aug. 1949.

Seated Woman. (1925). Lithograph from portfolio *Pierre Bonnard, peintre et lithographe,* 13 x 8 ½". The Museum of Modern Art, New York. Gift of Abby Aldrich Rockefeller

WORKS ILLUSTRATED BY BONNARD

* Asterisk indicates book in the Louis E. Stern Collection of Illustrated Books at The Museum of Modern Art.

JOZE, VICTOR, Reine de joie, moeurs du demi-monde. Paris, H. Julien, 1892. Lithograph (cover).

TERRASSE, CLAUDE. Petites scènes familières pour piano. Paris, Fromont, 1893. 19 lithographs and cover.

* TERRASSE, CLAUDE. Petit solfège illustré. Paris, Ancienne Maison Quantin, 1893. 30 lithographs and covers.

MELLERIO, ANDRÉ. La Lithographie originale en couleurs. Paris, L'Estampe et l'Affiche, 1898. 2 lithographs (cover and frontispiece).

* NANSEN, PETER, Marie. Paris, La Revue Blanche, 1898. 19 ink drawings (line cuts).

JARRY, ALFRED. Almanach du Père Ubu illustré. Paris, 1899. Ink drawings.

* COURTELINE, GEORGES and TERRASSE, CLAUDE. Pantheon-Courcelles. Paris, P. Dupont, (1900). Lithograph (cover and frontispiece).

* VERLAINE, PAUL. Parallèlement. Paris, Ambroise Vollard, 1900. 109 lithographs and 9 wood engravings.

* JARRY, ALFRED. Almanach illustré du Père Ubu pour le XXe siècle. Paris, 1901. 47 ink drawings (lithographs).

* LONGUS. Les Pastorales, ou Daphnis et Chloé. Paris, Ambroise Vollard, 1902. 151 lithographs.

BOYLESVE, RENÉ. La leçon d'amour dans un parc. Paris, La Revue Blanche, 1902. Cover.

RENARD, JULES. Histoires naturelles. Paris, Ernest Flammarion (1904). 67 ink drawings (line cuts).

* MIRBEAU, OCTAVE. La 628-E8. Paris, Charpentier et Fasquelle, 1908. 104 ink drawings (line cuts).

EBERHARDT, ISABELLE. Notes de route. Maroc—Algérie—Tunisie. 1908. 1 drawing by Bonnard (line cut).

BARRUCAND, VICTOR. D'un pays plus beau. Paris, Floury, 1910. 7 drawings.

GEFFROY, GUSTAVE. Preface to Germinal, album of prints. Paris, La Maison moderne, (c. 1910). 1 print by Bonnard.

MIRBEAU, OCTAVE and others. Cézanne. Paris, Bernheim Jeune, 1914. 1 lithograph by Bonnard after a Cézanne painting.

Catalogue of the Salon d'Automne. Paris. 1912. Cover.

* VOLLARD, AMBROISE. Le Père Ubu à l'hôpital. Paris, 1916. 2 ink drawings (line cuts).

* VOLLARD, AMBROISE. Le Père Ubu à l'aviation. Paris, Editions Georges Crés. 1918. 2 ink drawings (line cuts).

* GIDE, ANDRÉ. Der schlecht gefesselte Prometheus. Berlin, Hyperionverlag, 1919. 6 ink drawings (halftone).

* GIDE, ANDRÉ. Le Prométhée mal enchaîné. Paris, Nouvelle Revue Française, 1920. 30 drawings (line cuts).

ANET, CLAUDE. Notes sur l'amour. Paris, Crès, 1922. 14 drawings (engraved on wood by Yvonne Malliez).

* CHAUVEAU, LEOPOLD. Histoire du poisson scie et du poisson marteau. Paris, Payot, 1923. 38 drawings (line cuts).

GOMEZ DE LA SERNA, R. Seins. Paris, Crès, Les Cahiers d'Aujourd'hui, 1924. Drawings.

* MIRBEAU, OCTAVE. Dingo. Paris, Ambroise Vollard, 1924. 55 etchings.

FRAPIER, ed. Maîtres et petits maîtres d'aujourd'hui: Pierre Bonnard peintre et lithographe, text by C. Roger-Marx. Paris, Frapier, 1925. 4 lithographs.

* COQUIOT, GUSTAVE. En suivant la Seine. Paris, Delpeuch, 1926. 3 drawings.

* CHAUVEAU, LEOPOLD. Histoire du Petit Renaud. Paris, Nouvelle Revue Française, 1927. 49 drawings (pochoir).

TERRASSE, CLAUDE. Bonnard. Paris, Floury, 1927. 1 drypoint.

* Tableaux de Paris. Paris, Emile-Paul, 1927. 1 lithograph by Bonnard.

* ROGER-MARX, CLAUDE. Simili. Paris, Au Sans Pareil, 1930. 7 drypoints.

* VOLLARD, AMBROISE. La vie de Sainte Monique. Paris, Ambroise Vollard, 1930. 17 etchings, 29 drawings (transfer lithographs) and 178 woodcuts designed by Bonnard.

Paris 1937. Paris, Daragnes, 1937. 1 etching for BEDEL, MAURICE. "Faubourg Saint-Honoré."

* BONNARD, PIERRE. Correspondances. Paris, "Verve," ed. Tériade, 1944. 28 drawings (halftone).

* LOUYS, PIERRE. Le crepuscule des nymphes. Paris, Pierre Tisné, 1946. 24 lithographs.

COLETTE. Belles saisons. Paris, Club des lecteurs de la "Gazette des Lettres," 1947. Drawings.

VERVE. Couleur de Bonnard. Paris, "Verve," ed. Tériade, 1947. Cover, frontispiece, and all decorations designed by Bonnard.

FRONT COVER: Dining Room in the Country, Vernon. 1913. Oil, 64½ x 80″. The Minneapolis Institute of Art